The Sheep Knew

Written by Joann Benzinger and Patty Cornell
Illustrated by Joann Benzinger

AuthorHouse™
1663 Liberty Drive
Bloomington, IN 47403
www.authorhouse.com
Phone: 1 (800) 839-8640

Published by AuthorHouse: 03/27/2019

ISBN: 978-1-5246-4523-6 (sc)
ISBN: 978-1-5246-4524-3 (e)

Library of Congress Control Number: 2016917312

Print information available on the last page.

This book is printed on acid-free paper.

authorHOUSE®

The Sheep Knew

Written by Joann Benzinger
and Patty Cornell

DEDICATION

This book is dedicated to the little children around the world who need to know about the birth of Jesus Christ. It is also for the parents and others who will share the message of Christmas with those around them. Peace and Joy to all who read this book and may the spirit of the season be with you all year through.

*I*n that region there were shepherds living in the fields, keeping watch over their flock by night.

(Luke 2:8 NRSV)

Up on a hill in the bright star light
A flock of sheep lay watching the night.

Stars in the sky,
   twinkling with joy -

They know the secret
   of the Baby Boy!

$\mathscr{A}$nd suddenly there was with the angel a multitude of the heavenly host, praising God and saying,

"Glory to God in the highest heaven, and on earth peace among those whom he favors!"

(Luke 2:13, 14 NRSV)

Shepherds carefully watch the sheep
So much excitement -
no one can sleep.

Stars in the heavens
light up the sky,

Angels sing
"Glory to the Most High!"

*J*oseph also went from the town of
Nazareth in Galilee to Judea, to the city
of David called Bethlehem, because he
was descended from the house and
family of David.

(Luke 2:4 NRSV)

The donkey is tired, and Mary is, too.

Where can they sleep?

What will they do?

They come to Bethlehem -
a town so small,

The only room
is a donkey's stall.

*W*hile they were there, the time came for her to deliver her child.

(*Luke 2:6 NRSV*)

Cuddle beside the cows and the goats,
 The wonderful smell of hay and oats.

Joseph and Mary await His birth:
 This Child who will be the redemption of earth.

*T*n the time of King Herod, after Jesus was born in Bethlehem of Judea, wise men from the East came to Jerusalem.

(Matthew 2:1 NRSV)

A Baby named Jesus, this Gift from above -
A Child to show us the Father's Love.

Over the stable the star shines bright
Marking the birthplace -

"O, Holy Night!"

When they saw that the star had stopped,
they were overwhelmed with joy.
(Matthew 2:10 NRSV)

By the star in the sky the wise men are led
To the Baby Jesus' bed.

Precious gifts they give with joy
To the new born Baby boy.

A light for the world -
The Bright Morning Star!

No need to wonder at all
who You are!

*B*ut you, Bethlehem Ephrathah,
   Though you are little among
      the thousands of Judah,
  Yet out of you shall come forth to Me
  The One to be Ruler in Israel,
  Whose goings forth are from of old,
    From everlasting."

                     (Micah 5:2 NKJV)

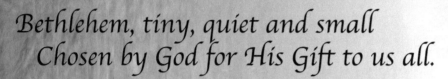

Bethlehem, tiny, quiet and small
Chosen by God for His Gift to us all.

Who could have guessed it?
Who else knew?

The stars and the sheep did,
And now you do, too!

This story can be presented as a children's play. The following suggestions can be helpful when using it as a Christmas Pageant.

Characters needed:

- Readers-preferably one older and one younger
- 2 Shepherds and multiple sheep
- 2 or more Angels
- Mary, Joseph, and a donkey
- 3 Wisemen with gifts
- One Child holding a bright star
- Additional animals as children are available

The stage and equipment:

There is a stable with a manger in it on the stage.

There should be space on both sides of the stable for children. Children enter the stage area from both the left or right as indicated.

The shepherds with their sheep enter on the right. The Angels enter second also on the right. Mary, Joseph, and the donkey enter from the left. The Wisemen enter from the left also.

If possible, there should be risers for the angels behind the sheep on the right side of the stage. There should also be a holder for the star on the stable.

Songs are suggested. Children should sing the number of verses that they are able to do. All hymns are public domain.

Reader 1: In that region There were Shepherds living in the fields, keeping watch over their flock by night.

Actions: Two Shepherds bring their flock of sheep onto the stage from the right side. Sheep look to the sky.

Reader 2: Up on a hill in the bright star light, a flock of sheep lay watching the night. Stars in the sky, twinkling with joy. They know the secret of the Baby Boy!

Song: It Came Upon a Midnight Clear

Reader 1: And suddenly there was with the angels a multitude of the heavenly host, praising God and saying, "Glory to God in the Highest heaven, and on earth peace among those whom he favors."

Actions: The angels appear on the right and move up on the risers behind the Shepherd and sheep.

Reader 2: Shepherds carefully watch the sheep. So much excitement, no one can sleep. Stars in the heavens light up the sky, Angels sing "Glory to the Most High!"

Song: Angels We Have Heard on High

Reader 1: Joseph also went from the town of Nazareth in Galilee to Judea, to the city of David called Bethlehem, because he was descended from the house and family of David.

Actions: Mary, Joseph, with a donkey enter the stage from the left. They look to the stable which is located center stage.

Reader 2: The donkey is tired, and Mary is too. Where can they sleep? What will they do? They come to Bethlehem, a town so small, the only room is a donkey's stall.

Song: Oh, Little Town of Bethlehem

Reader 1: While they were there, the time came for her to deliver her child.

Actions: Mary and Joseph move towards the stable and kneel near the manger. Mary takes the baby Jesus from behind the Manger and wraps him in a blanket. She then lays him in the manger to sleep.

Reader 2: Cuddle beside the cows and the goats, the wonderful smell of hay and oats, Joseph and Mary await His birth: This child who will be the redemption of earth.

Song: Away in a Manger

Reader 1: In the time of King Herod, after Jesus was born in Bethlehem of Judea, wise men from the East came to Jerusalem.

Actions: The Wisemen enter from the left looking around. They are holding gifts.

Reader 2: A baby named Jesus, this gift from above- A child to show us the Father's Love. Over the stable the star shines bright marking the birthplace! Oh, Holy Night!

Song: Oh, Holy Night sung by an adult choir if possible

Reader 1: When they saw that the star had stopped, they were overwhelmed with joy.

Actions: The child holding a 'bright' star enters from either side and puts the star on the stable. The Wisemen move closer to the manger, looking at the baby, they kneel.

Reader 2: By the star in the sky the wise men are led to the Baby Jesus' bed. Precious gifts they give with joy to the new born Baby boy. A light for the world, the bright morning star! No need to wonder at all who you are!

Song: Joy to the World

Reader 1: But you, Bethlehem Ephrathah, though you are little among the thousands of Judah, yet out of you shall come forth to Me the One to be Ruler in Israel, whose goings forth are from of old from everlasting.

Actions: The sheep move to the front of the stage and look adoringly at the baby Jesus. Shepherds and Wisemen move in closer to see the baby.

Reader 2: Bethlehem, tiny, quiet and small Chosen by God for His gift to us all. Who could have guessed it? Who else knew? The stars and the sheep did, and now you do too!

The children can face forward and stand in a choir formation with Mary located in the center holding the Baby Jesus.

Song: Silent Night

Children remain in place while the close is read.

Close (read by Reader 1)…. "But really, what more can you say?"

If you were there, what would you say? How about Thank You? When we ponder what the birth of Christ really means to each and every one of us, 'thank you' seems like the most appropriate response. So, let us pray:

Thank you, Dear Heavenly Father for sending us your precious Son, that He might be born into this world, so that we may hold onto the hope of spending our eternity with You in Your Heavenly Kingdom.

Thank you for the many blessings we have in our Faith Family, that the children can sing, that the Choir can lift up your praises, and we can together sing your songs of joy proclaiming the message of Christmas.

We look back to the night when Jesus was born and wonder who knew? And who believed? Would we have believed? Strengthen our faith that we know with confidence and proclaim the message loudly with the Angels on high "Christ is Born!" Celebrate the Season with Joy in your heart! And together we say, "Amen."

All Suggested Songs are Public Domain

It Came Upon a Midnight Clear sung by the children

It came upon a midnight clear,
That glorious song of old.
From angels playing near the earth
To touch their harps of gold.

Peace on the Earth, goodwill to men
From Heaven's all-gracious King.
The world in solemn stillness lay
To hear the angels sing.

Gloria – Angels We Have Heard on High sung by the children

Angels we have heard on high,
Sweetly singing o're the plains,
And the mountains in reply,
Echoing their joyous strains.

Gloria in excelsis Deo sung by ALL
Gloria in excelsis Deo

Oh, little town of Bethlehem sung by the children

Oh little town of Bethlehem, how still we see Thee lie,
Above thy deep and dreamless sleep the silent stars go by.
Yet in the dark streets shineth the everlasting light,
The hopes and fears of all the years are met in thee tonight.

Away in a Manger sung by the children

Away in a manger,
No crib for His bed,
The little Lord Jesus
Laid down His sweet head.

The stars in the bright sky
Looked down where He lay.
The little Lord Jesus,
Asleep on the hay.

The cattle are lowing,
The poor Baby wakes,
But little Lord Jesus
No crying He makes.

I love Thee, Lord Jesus
Look down from the sky,
And stay by my cradle,
'Til morning is nigh.

Joy to the World, The Lord has come!

[Verse 1] sung by children
Joy to the world, the Lord has come!
Let earth receive her King;
Let every heart prepare Him room,
And Heaven and nature sing,
And Heaven and nature sing,
And Heaven, and Heaven, and nature sing.

[Verse 2] sung by all
Joy to the world, the Savior reigns!
Let men their songs employ,
While fields and floods, rocks, hills and plains
Repeat the sounding joy,
Repeat the sounding joy,
Repeat, repeat, the sounding joy.

Silent Night

[Verse 1] Sung by Children
Silent night, holy night!
All is calm, all is bright.
Round yon Virgin, Mother and Child,
Holy Infant, so tender and mild.
Sleep in heavenly peace.
Sleep in heavenly peace.

[Verse 2] Sung with Choir
Silent night, holy night!
Shepherds quake at the sight.
Glories stream from heaven afar.
Heavenly hosts sing Alleluia!
Christ the Savior is born.
Christ the Savior is born.

[Verse 3] Sung with All
Silent night, holy night!
Son of God, love's pure light.
Radiant beams from Thy holy face,
With dawn of redeeming grace,
Jesus Lord, at Thy birth.
Jesus Lord, at Thy birth.

First Verse can be repeated.

Printed in the United States
By Bookmasters